PIECING

the Piece O' Cake Way

- 15 Skill-Building Projects / 27 Quilts
- Today's Guide to Quilting Basics
- Color Choices Made Easy

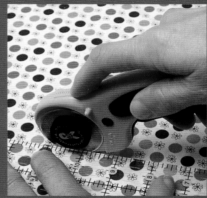

Becky Goldsmith and Linda Jenkins

C&T PUBLISHING

Text and Artwork copyright © 2007 by Becky Goldsmith and Linda Jenkins

Artwork copyright © 2007 by C&T Publishing, Inc.

Publisher: Amy Marson

Editorial Director: Gailen Runge

Acquisitions Editor: Jan Grigsby

Editor: Lynn Koolish

Technical Editors: Teresa Stroin and Amanda Siegfried

Copyeditor/Proofreader: Wordfirm Inc.

Cover Designer/Book Designer: Kristen Yenche

Illustrators: Becky Goldsmith and Tim Manibusan

Production Coordinator: Zinnia Heinzmann

Photography by C&T Publishing, Inc., unless otherwise noted

Published by C&T Publishing, Inc., P.O. Box 1456, Lafayette, CA 94549

Library of Congress Cataloging-in-Publication Data

Goldsmith, Becky.
  Piecing the piece o' cake way : 15 skill-building projects, 27 quilts, today's guide to quilting basics, color choices made easy / Becky Goldsmith and Linda Jenkins.
    p. cm.
  Includes index.
  ISBN-13: 978-1-57120-416-5 (paper trade : alk. paper)
  ISBN-10: 1-57120-416-4 (paper trade : alk. paper)
  1. Patchwork—Patterns. 2. Quilting—Patterns. I. Jenkins, Linda. II. Title.

TT835.G6547 2007
746.46'041—dc22

                                        2007017741

Printed in China

10 9 8 7 6 5 4 3 2 1

Acknowledgments

We've said it before, and we'll say it again—we are very lucky to be associated with C&T! Everyone there has been very good to us. First, Todd Hensley, CEO, welcomed us with open arms. Amy Marson, publisher, is always there to support us. Lynn Koolish, our editor, helps us to make each book the best it can be. We thank them all.

It would be nice to be perfect, but we aren't, so we are very grateful to Teresa Stroin, our technical editor, who makes sure that we get the details right. Luke Mulks and Diane Pedersen, our photographers, make everything look beautiful. Kris Yenche, this book's designer, has given *Piecing the Piece O' Cake Way* its cheerful and happy appearance. We thank you all for your excellent efforts.

Three women helped us make the quilts in this book. Elsie Ridgley and Diane Redfearn helped us make several quilt tops. Mary Covey machine quilted many of the quilts in this book. We appreciate their excellent efforts!

Dedication

FROM BECKY

Janette Meetze was my first quilting teacher, at the Cotton Patch quilt shop in Tulsa, Oklahoma. She made quite an impression on me! Her six-week sampler class was well thought out. She was always prepared, and she was unfailingly helpful to each student. When I teach now, I always try to do as good a job as Janette did.

Janette taught us the basics of quilting in that class. I certainly felt capable to go out and tackle any quilt I took a notion to make. Every quilter should be so lucky.

Thank you, Janette!

FROM LINDA

Betty Crowell was my first quilting teacher, in 1983. Her class was before rotary tools. Everything was hand pieced, and the patterns were traced onto the fabric using a template. We used a $\frac{1}{4}''$ tool to add our seam allowances.

Our home was flooded in 1984. All of my hand-pieced blocks were soaked. I was able to save most of them. Two years later, I went to the Cotton Patch quilt shop in Tulsa, Oklahoma, with my blocks in hand. I asked if they offered a sampler class that I could sit in on so I could finish my quilt. Betty Terrell was teaching a sampler class using rotary tools.

I was blessed to have had the opportunity to learn the basics from Betty Crowell who taught me hand piecing and Betty Terrell who taught the basics using rotary tools. These two ladies gave me a firm foundation in quiltmaking.

Often quilters begin by making a quilt with specific techniques using a tool made for that pattern. It is our hope in writing this book that you learn the basics you need to tackle any quilt.

Thank you, Betty Crowell and Betty Terrell.

12. Pin the joined ends to the quilt, and finish sewing the binding to the quilt.

13. Turn the binding to the back of the quilt, covering the raw edges. If there is too much batting, trim some to leave your binding nicely filled. Hand stitch the folded edge of the binding to the back of the quilt. Hand stitch the mitered corner edges down on the back and the front.

 Did You Know?

MAKING PERFECT BINDING CORNERS

Holice Turnbow shared with us this variation on binding corners. If you have trouble seeing where to stop sewing at the corner for your backstitch, try this technique. Fold the binding at a 45° angle, and pin before you get to the corner, as shown. This creates an accurate diagonal fold line.

Stop sewing when you reach this diagonal fold line, and backstitch. If your seam allowance is accurate, you will make your backstitch at the correct spot for any width binding.

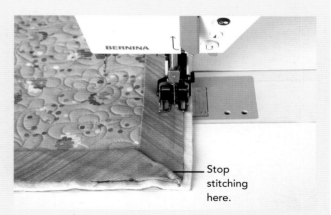

Stop stitching here.

Now, refold the binding as shown in Steps 7 and 8 (on page 30), and begin sewing the next side of the quilt.

TRIMMING THE CORNERS OF THE BATTING

Turning the mitered corners of the binding to the back of the quilt can be cumbersome. A trick is to trim the batting and backing at a 45° angle. Doing so alleviates some of the bulk.

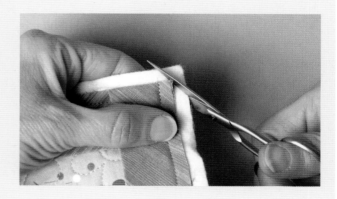

MAKING A LABEL

It is important that you make a fabric label and sew it to the back of the quilt. Include information that you want people to know about the quilt. Your name and address, the date, the fiber content of the quilt and batting, and whether it was made for a special person or occasion are all things you can write on the label.

Your label can be plain or fancy, embroidered or written with a permanent pen. You can use a photo transfer to add images. You can add appliqué or other embellishments. Use your imagination! Make sure that your label will withstand laundering. Heat set any written information.

Some quilters like to attach the label to the quilt back before quilting. If the label is quilted into the quilt it is very difficult to remove, thus ensuring that the information stays with the quilt. However, the quilting threads can be unsightly and can make the label more difficult to read.

Label on back of *Colorful Coins*

SIGNING YOUR QUILT

We have come to the conclusion that it's a good idea to get your name onto the front of your quilt as well as putting a label on the back. You can do so in a variety of ways.

You can embroider or appliqué your name or initials and the date on the quilt top. You can add this information with a permanent pen. Or you can quilt your name and the date into your quilt with matching or contrasting thread. Regardless of how you do it, be sure to do it!

Becky's signature and year quilted into *Colorful Coins*

Strips

Working from strips of fabric is a fast, efficient, and accurate way to piece.

For most quilts, you cut strips first. Then you cut shapes from those strips. Squares, for example, are usually cut from strips. It is important to learn to cut strips accurately before moving on to other shapes.

CUTTING STRIPS

If you haven't read the rotary cutting instructions on pages 16–18, please do so now.

pages 16–18

Did You Know?

Fabric off the bolt is 40″ wide or wider. When you are instructed to cut strips 40″ long, it most often means that you are to cut strips the full width of the fabric. It's okay if your strip is longer than that. However, if your strip is shorter than that, it may not be long enough, and you may need to cut another strip. Read through the instructions before you begin cutting.

USING A ROTARY CUTTING MAT
Lines on cutting mats are not always accurate for precise cutting. Rely only on the lines on your ruler. We use the blank side of our cutting mat more often than the lined side.

1. To cut a strip, place the fabric, folded with selvages together with the fold nearest you, on your mat. Make sure that the fabric is smooth. Place the ruler on the fabric, lining up the 1″ line with the fold in the fabric. Cut away the excess fabric on the right side of the ruler. (Left-handers, arrange the fabric to cut from the other side of the ruler.)

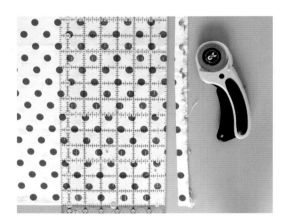

2. Carefully rotate your mat, or you may choose to flip over the fabric so that the cut edge is on the left. In either case, be sure that the folded edge and the cut edge remain straight and aligned.

3. You are going to cut a 2½″-wide strip. This strip will be the length of the fabric—40″ long. Find the 2½″ marks on the ruler. Remember that some rulers have an extra ½″ on one side—be sure that you are reading the ruler correctly. Place the 2½″ marks on the cut line. Look all the way down the length of the ruler. Don't let the ruler angle out of position. Keep the 1″ line even with the fold in the fabric.

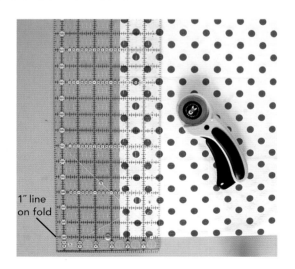

1″ line on fold

4. Cut the strip.

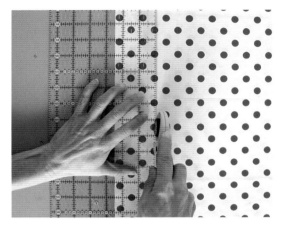

5. Open the strip, and check to be sure that it is straight. If your strip is V-shaped, it means that the 1″ line on your ruler was not lined up correctly with the fold in the fabric. If that is the case, you need to begin again at Step 1.

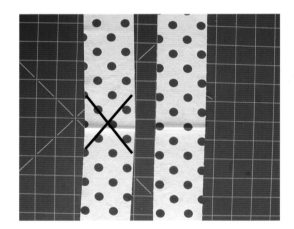

6. If you need to cut more strips, continue as described above. After you cut 2 or 3 strips, check to be sure that the cut edge is still square with the ruler and perpendicular to the fold. It is very easy to angle your ruler just a little with each cut. The more strips you cut, the more this edge can angle. If your cut edge is no longer square with the ruler, rotate the fabric, and re-square it as in Step 1.

7. Cut all strips in this manner.

8. Keep like kinds and sizes of strips together, and label them by size or use. You may think you'll remember exactly what you cut and why, but that's often not the case—ask us how we know!

CUTTING STRIPS WIDER THAN YOUR RULER

You can use more than one ruler at a time. When cutting strips wider than your ruler, place two rulers side by side. Pay attention to your addition—be sure that you are cutting strips of the correct size. Once the rulers are in position on the fabric, hold onto the ruler closest to the cut.

CUTTING STRIP LENGTHS

Long Strips

For the Chinese Coins quilts that follow, you'll need several strips 6½″ × 39½″. First cut the fabric 6½″ wide × 40″, across the width of the fabric. Fold this strip in half. To determine the size to cut the folded strip, divide 39½″ by 2 to get 19¾″. Place the ruler on the fold at the 19¾″ mark. Be sure that the long edge of the ruler is lined up with a cut edge of the strip. Cut away the excess fabric.

Short Strips

The Log Cabin quilts in this book require strips in a variety of lengths. To make it easier, you can cut many strips at a time.

1. When you need to cut many strips of a certain length, you can stack strips or place strips side by side—or both. Just be sure to keep the strips straight and the strip edges even with one another. When you cut, align the marks on the *ruler* with the cut edges of the strips. This is a good time to use the lines on your cutting mat to help you keep the strips straight.

2. Cut off the selvages at the ends of the strip. Be sure to cut them off at a 90° angle. (Left-handers, cut from the other side of the strip.)

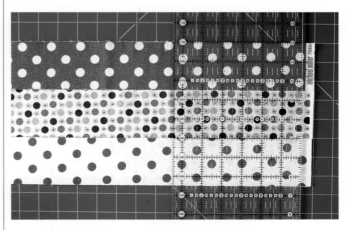

3. Rotate the mat and strips (so you don't have to move the strips). Place your ruler on the strips, and cut the lengths indicated in the pattern.

4. After you cut 2 or 3 strips, check to be sure that the end cut edge is still square with the ruler. If it is not, square it up before continuing.

5. Continue cutting strips until you have the number of strips indicated in the pattern.

Remember that when cutting through many thicknesses, you need to be especially careful not to angle your rotary cutter. Keep your cutter perpendicular to the mat so that all strips are cut the same width, and keep a firm grip on the ruler.

Chinese Coins

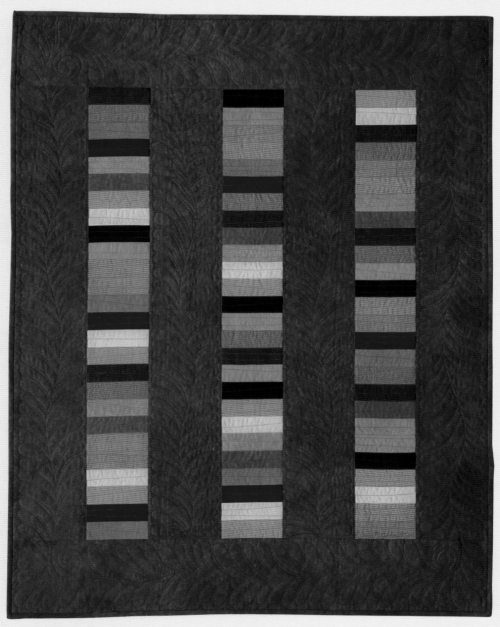

COLORFUL COINS
made by Becky Goldsmith

The solid fabrics in this quilt really show off the quilted feathers. In nature, colors in the distance are often grayer, and colors that are closer to you are clearer and brighter. The bold, clear colors in the bars appear to come forward, and the grayer, blue fabric recedes.

 Finished quilt size: 39″ × 51″

The Chinese Coins pattern is a bar quilt. The name refers to the vertical strips that look like bars. The Chinese Coins are the stacked horizontal strips in the pieced bars. This quilt is very easy to make and a great place to begin working on an accurate ¼″ seam allowance.

3. Use a positioning pin to match the dots at the far end of the curved seams. Turn the inner curve fabric to line up the outer edges of the 2 fabrics.

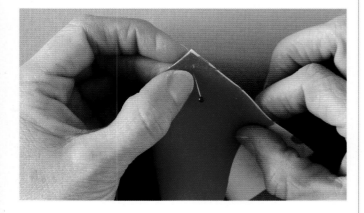

4. Pin the shapes together just to the right of the positioning pin. Remove the positioning pin.

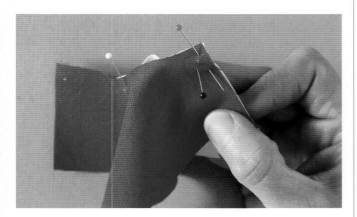

5. Repeat at the other end of the curved seam.

6. You may need more than 3 pins. If so, ease the inner curve to fit the outer curve, matching raw edges.

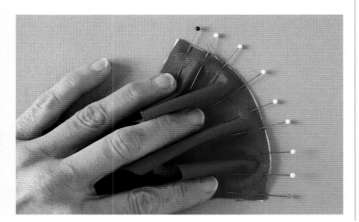

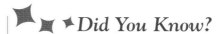

Did You Know?

SEWING CURVES

It is often easier to distribute the fabric evenly on curves if the fabric is pinned while being held flat against a hard surface. First pin the center and ends of the curve as described above.

With your left hand, hold the piece with the outer curve flat against your rotary mat or tabletop. With your right hand, gently work the piece with the inner curve into position. Do not pull or stretch the fabric out of shape. Use as many pins as you need.

CLIPPING CURVES

Most curves tend to fall on the bias grain of the fabric. Bias edges stretch easier than those on the straight of grain. Because these edges are stretchy, you are less likely to need to clip seams.

Clipped seam allowances are weaker, so we do our best to avoid clipping curves. However, you may need to clip inner curves if you press the seam allowances back toward the inner curve and the fabric won't stretch enough to press flat. If your curve is cut on the straight of grain, you may need to clip.

Clip only inner curves. Never clip outer curves. Always sew a test block to see if you must clip before you begin snipping away.

SEWING CURVES

1. Place the pinned pieces in your sewing machine. Keep the bottom outer curved piece flat against the bed of the machine.

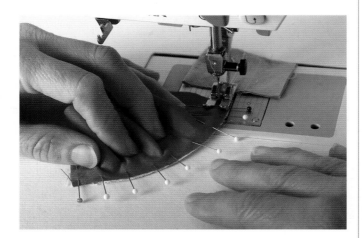

2. Begin sewing. Use your right hand to manipulate the top, inner curve into position. Remove pins as necessary.

3. *Sew slowly, and follow the curve.* Let the fabric slowly rotate into position.

4. Finger-press the seam flat against the ironing board, then press with the iron. Press the seam allowance toward the darker fabric. However, if the seam allowance of the inner curve won't stretch open without clipping, you may want to press the block toward the lighter fabric so that the inner curve lies flat. Doing so reduces the need for clipping the inner curve. Your block should now measure $4\frac{1}{2}'' \times 4\frac{1}{2}''$.

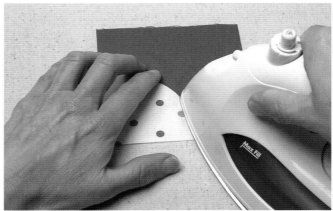

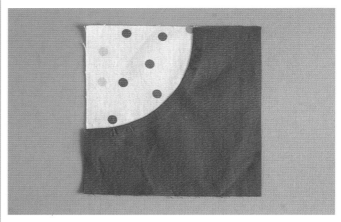

5. Practice sewing curves on the remaining pieces.

Drunkard's Path

DRUNKARD'S PATH FLOWERS
made by Becky Goldsmith

Fabric from the 1930s has a distinctive look. The colors are clear, but soft. The prints tend to be small scale, but there are exceptions.

You can find antique fabric that was made in the 1930s, as well as new reproduction fabric. You can find current fabric that is neither antique nor reproduction but still has a flavor of 1930s fabric. The best part about these fabrics is that they almost always look good together—no matter how you combine them—as long as you pay attention to value placement. Here, the many colors stand out against the field of light yellow.

Finished quilt size: 46″ × 46″

Both of these quilts are made with the same number of blocks. You can make a wide variety of designs with this simple Drunkard's Path block. It's a lot of fun to play with on your design wall.

Window fabric

K: Cut 1 strip 2″ × 40″; then cut 18 squares 2″ × 2″.

L: Cut 1 strip 1½″ × 40″; then cut 9 squares 1½″ × 1½″.

Door fabric

R: Cut 1 strip 2″ × 4″ from each of 9 fabrics for a total of 9 strips.

Chimney fabric

T: Cut 9 squares 1½″ × 1½″ from a variety of house fabric scraps.

Grass fabric

S: Cut 3 strips 1½″ × 40″; then cut 9 strips 1½″ × 9½″.

Fence fabric

U: Cut 36 strips 1″ × 4½″ in matching sets of 3 from a variety of house fabric scraps.

Red inner border fabric

Cut 5 strips 1½″ × 40″.

Brown outer border and horizontal sashing fabric

Outer border: Cut 5 strips 3½″ × 40″.

Sashing: Cut 3 strips 2½″ × 40″.

Binding fabric

(Refer to pages 28–29 for making continuous bias.)

Cut 1 square 23″ × 23″ to make a 2½″-wide continuous bias strip at least 209″ long.

BLOCKS

Make one block at a time. Doing so helps you to keep the fabrics for each house together. Refer to pages 58–60 for the instructions to make triangle-squares.

1. Make a triangle-square from background M and roof front I 3½″ × 3½″ squares. Press the seam allowances toward the darker fabric.

2. Make a triangle-square from roof front I and roof side J 3½″ × 3½″ squares. Press the seam allowances toward the darker fabric.

3. Make a triangle-square from roof side J and background M 3½″ × 3½″ squares. Press the seam allowances toward the darker fabric.

4. Sew 4 background Q strips alternately with 3 fence U strips, 1″ × 4½″ each. Press the seam allowances toward the darker fabric.

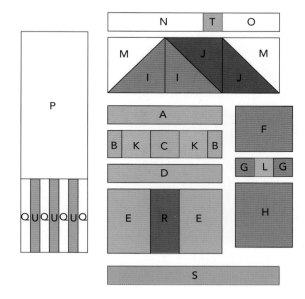

5. Refer to the diagram above, and assemble the House block units on your design wall.

6. Sew 2 of house front B, 2 of window K, and 1 of house front C together into a row. Press the seam allowances toward the house front fabric.

7. Sew a house front E to each side of door R. Press the seam allowances toward the house front fabric.

8. Sew the house front rows together. Press the seam allowances toward house front strips A and D.

9. Sew a house side G square to each side of window L. Press the seam allowances toward the house side fabric.

10. Sew the house side rows together. Press the seam allowances toward house sides F and H.

11. Sew the house front and house side together. Press the seam allowances toward the house front.

12. Sew the 3 roof triangle-squares together. Press the seam allowances toward the darker fabric.

13. Sew background N and background O to chimney T. Press the seam allowances toward the chimney.

14. Sew the chimney row to the roof row. Press the seam allowances toward the chimney row.

15. Sew the roof to the house. Press the seam allowances toward the roof.

16. Sew grass S to the house. Press the seam allowances toward the grass.

17. Sew background P to the fence unit. Press the seam allowances toward the background.

18. Sew the fence and the house together. Press the seam allowances toward the house. Your House block should now measure 13″ × 12½″.

EXTRA FENCE UNITS

1. Sew 4 background Q strips alternately with 3 fence U strips, 1″ × 4½″ each. Press the seam allowances toward the darker fabric.

2. Sew background P to the Q/U fence unit. Press the seam allowances toward the background.

3. Repeat Steps 1 and 2 to make a total of 3 extra fence units.

HORIZONTAL SASHING

1. Cut off the selvages from both ends of the 3 horizontal sashing strips.

2. Sew the strips end to end, right sides together. Press the seam allowances in one direction.

3. Cut 2 strips 2½″ × 41½″.

INNER BORDER

As with all quilts, it is a good idea to measure through the center of your pieced quilt to verify the width and length before you cut the inner border strips.

1. Cut off the selvages from both ends of the 5 inner border strips.

2. Sew the strips end to end, right sides together. Press the seam allowances in one direction.

3. Cut 2 strips 1½″ × 40½″ for the side inner borders.

4. Cut 2 strips 1½″ × 43½″ for the top and bottom inner borders.

OUTER BORDER

As with all quilts, it is a good idea to measure through the center of your pieced quilt to verify the width and length before you cut the outer border strips.

1. Cut off the selvages from both ends of the 5 border strips.

2. Sew the strips end to end, right sides together. Press the seam allowances in one direction.

3. Cut 2 strips 3½″ × 42½″ for the side outer borders.

4. Cut 2 strips 3½″ × 49½″ for the top and bottom outer borders.

SPARK UP THE BORDER WITH STRIPS OF COLOR!

Linda inserted strips of colorful fabric into her borders. To do so, cut 24 strips 1½″ × 3½″ from a variety of fabrics. Next, cut each border strip in 6 places. Space these cuts randomly. Sew a strip of fabric into each cut. Press the seam allowances toward the colorful inserted strip. Once all of the strips are sewn in, cut your borders to the lengths listed in Outer Border, Steps 3 and 4, above.